Finance Made Easy
(2nd Edition)

Les Livingstone MBA, Ph.D. CPA (NY & TX)

D0169809

3

Finance Made Easy (2nd Edition)

Dedication

To Trudy, with love.

Finance Made Easy (2nd Edition)

Life can only be understood backwards;
but it must be lived forwards.
Soren Kierkegaard

5

Preface

Why do we need this book? There are plenty of books on financial management, so what is different about this one? Good question. This book is as simple and as straight to the point as possible. It uses a practical, down-to-earth approach, and it is concise. All of the essentials are covered, in an easy-to understand style, with lots of examples and a summary at the end of each chapter. Further, this book bases all finance calculations on Microsoft Excel, which is the planet's best number cruncher, used by financial professionals worldwide. This book has everything you need, but nothing more. That's why we need this book.

6

Finance Made Easy (2nd Edition)

Table of Contents

Chapter 1

Risk and Return

It's not what you look at that
matters, it's what you see.

Henry David Thoreau

Financial executives are reputed to be much
too cautious because risk is inherent in
business, as it is in life itself. As the saying
goes "faint heart never won fair lady[1]." But
for every saying, there is another saying
with the exact opposite meaning. For
example "look before you leap." Let us

---

[1] Miguel de Cervantes.

simply say that an auto needs both good acceleration and good brakes.

While some risks are unavoidable, other risks are unwarranted or preventable. So the wise course seems to be taking worthwhile risks, but averting unnecessary risks. But how do we tell which risks may be unavoidable, and which may be unwarranted? Answering that important question is a major part of finance. In brief, the answer is to avoid risks when the odds of success are poor, and when the rewards of success seem small. By the same token, risks are worthwhile when the odds of success are favorable, and the rewards of success seem generous. These concepts lead us to exploring (a) the relationship between risk and reward, and (b) how to measure the magnitude of risk.

Risk and Reward

All large companies started out as small, risky enterprises. What they have in common is winning large rewards in terms of success. The large, successful companies are easy to see. What is difficult to see is the huge number of firms that failed. They fell by the wayside, and disappeared without a trace.

We often hear that risk and reward are linked together, so that the greater the risk, the greater the reward. But that is only a half-truth. More accurately, the greater the risk, the greater the chance of reward. But if risk is greater, outcomes are less certain. Therefore the greater the risk, the greater the uncertainty of the outcome. So the correct relation of risk to reward is that the greater the risk, the greater the rewards of success and the greater the penalties of failure.

In other words, the greater the risk, the greater the rewards for success and the greater the penalties for failure, but the more uncertain the outcome. So its not only true that greater risk carries greater reward, but greater risk also carries greater penalties for failure. And greater risk may increase the size of both rewards and penalties, but it lowers the likelihood of winning a reward or incurring a penalty. For example, the top prize in a state lottery is a huge sum, but the chance of winning the top prize is remote.

We have learned the following:

	High Risk	Low Risk
High Probability		Small Reward or Penalty
Low Probability	Large Reward or Penalty	

As the table shows, the higher the risk, the larger the reward or penalty, but the lower the probability of obtaining either reward or penalty. By the same token, the lower the risk, the smaller the reward or penalty, but the higher the probability of obtaining either reward or penalty. For example, in the game

11

of baseball, there is a higher probability of hitting a single, and a lower probability of hitting a home run. In business there is a higher probability of earning a 3% return with low risk, and a lower probability of earning a 30% return with greater risk.

Measuring Risk

Since risk is related to return, it is important to measure risk. One way to measure risk is to use what statisticians call a "standard deviation." A standard deviation describes the range of values that a variable might cover. For example, a manufacturer of ladies clothing may need statistics of how tall most women are. According to the National Center for Health Statistics, the average height for an adult female in the United States is 63.8 inches, or 5 feet 3.8 inches. Of course, some women are taller, and some are shorter than average.

The average tells us that most of the women were somewhere around 63.8 inches tall.

But there were deviations from the average. The standard deviation tells how big these deviations were. The standard deviation says how far away numbers in a list typically are from their average. Most values in the list will be within one standard deviation (2.5 inches) of the average. Very few values will be more than two or three standard deviations away from the average.

When a variable is normally distributed (so that the frequency distribution is bell-shaped), roughly 68% of the entries on a list (around two thirds) are within one standard deviation of the average (including both directions), the other 32% are further away. Roughly 95% (19 in 20) are within two standard deviations of the average, the other 5% are further away. Many variables are more or less normally distributed, so this rule of thumb works for most lists of numbers, though not all.

So a general concept of risk is the standard deviation, for variables that have been measured. Of course, not all variables have been measured, and not all variables can be measured. For example, insurance companies have very good statistics on fires, burglaries, auto accidents, and human longevity. Electric utility companies have excellent data on power usage by industrial, commercial, municipal, and household customers. But some variables are simply not measurable – for example no-one knows where the next hurricane or tornado might hit. Also no-one knows where the next terrorist attack might happen, or what harm it might do.

So for variables that are not regular in occurrence, there may be no averages or standard deviations. In those cases, there is ample uncertainty, to be sure, but no way to measure their uncertainty. It is helpful to distinguish between risk and uncertainty. We can define risk as applying to variables that are regular in occurrence, and where there are data and averages and standard deviations. In contrast, we define uncertainty as applying to variables that are irregular in occurrence, and where there are no reliable data and no reliable averages or standard deviations. Therefore we can use standard deviations to measure risk, but we have no measure when it comes to uncertainty.

Risk Reduction

One obvious method of risk reduction is simply to avoid taking any chances. But refusing to take any chances is highly impractical. If all businesses simply invested their resources in relatively safe government securities, then no goods or services would be provided. Neither Bill Gates, nor Steve Jobs, nor Warren Buffett got rich by shrinking away from risk. All businesses must take risks in order to succeed. At the same time, most businesses follow risk reduction strategies such as reducing sales volatility, minimizing fixed costs, purchasing insurance, and diversification.

Firms often reduce sales volatility and spread fixed costs by practicing market segmentation. For example, seasonal resorts offer off-season discounts, airlines offer low-price standby fares, restaurants offer "early bird" dinners, bars and taverns offer "happy hours" and "ladies nights," cinemas and theatres offer matinees, and many businesses offer student discounts and senior discounts.

Most businesses purchase insurance to protect themselves from hazards such as fire, flood, and legal liability to customers, to staff, and to bystanders. But there are some risks that cannot be insured against – for instance, the risk of failure or bankruptcy.

One protection against the risk of failure or bankruptcy is diversification. The diversification might take the form of multiple lines of business. For example in the past some firms sold coal in winter and ice in summer. Also in the past, a merchant might prefer to own a 10% interest in 10 different sailing ships, rather than owning a 100% interest in just one sailing ship. Some golf clubs offer golf in spring and summer, with cross country skiing in fall and winter. Some businesses diversify geographically by opening branches in various locations. Similarly, freight carriers might have several different routes, airlines might fly to multiple destinations, and railroads might team up with truckers and ship lines to offer multimodal transportation.

Despite these risk-reduction strategies, risk is unavoidable and omnipresent. So firms may also seek extra compensation for assuming risk. For example, supermarkets tend to have very low profit margins because they sell many necessities, such as foods, that sell in good times and in bad times. But jewelers and book publishers tend to have very high profit margins because they sell goods that are not commonly accepted as necessities, and which can easily be postponed or simply not purchased at all.

Another way to compensate for risk is in the rate of return required to invest in various projects. For example, it may be acceptable to replace an old machine with a similar new version at a fairly modest rate of return. But a project to introduce a new and different product may only be considered at a much higher required rate of return. Similarly, introducing an existing product into a new market may only be considered at a much higher required rate of return than for expanding an existing product into an existing market.

Linking Risk and Return

The Capital Asset Pricing Model (CAPM) is a method of calculating the required return on an asset according to its risk. The CAPM formula is:

$$k = RF + (M - RF)\beta$$

where k = the required rate of return,

and RF = the risk-free rate of return,

and M = the rate of return on the entire market,

and β = the project beta,

and (M − RF) = the risk premium.

For example, with RF = 2%, M = 8%, β = 1.9, and (M − RF) = 6%, then

$$k = 2\% + 6\% \times 1.9 = 13.4\%$$

and if we change β to 0.8, then the required rate of return, k becomes:

$$k = 2\% + 6\% \times 0.8 = 6.8\%$$

Plainly k is sensitive to β, the measure of risk based on standard deviation. The other components of k are RF (the risk-free rate of return) and M (the rate of return on the entire market). These rates of return or rates of interest are made up of three components.

What Is Beta?

The variable β represents risk. For example, for the entire stock market, β is standardized as 1.0. Therefore stocks with below-average risk have betas less than one. Examples of these lower-risk stocks are public utilities and food-producer stocks because they supply necessities which are purchased in bad times as well as good times. Stocks with above-average risk have betas greater than one. Examples of these higher-risk stocks are producers of recreational items, such as golf clubs, skis, and tennis rackets, which sell much better in good times than bad times.

The Components of Interest Rates

The risk-free rate of return must include an amount for delaying consumption, because delaying consumption is what lenders and other investors are compelled to do. In order to provide an incentive to delay consumption, the risk-free rate of return must include an amount to compensate for delaying consumption.

There must also be an allowance for inflation. Inflation is more money chasing fewer goods, or – if you like – a reduction in the purchasing power of money. In the past, the gold standard constrained the creation of money to the amount of gold available. But the gold standard was junked about halfway through the 20th century. Today, without the constraint of a gold standard, and with paper money, governments are free to print as many paper money units as they wish. So governments are free to generate as much inflation as they wish.

Moreover, governments have an incentive to print paper money. For one thing, with progressive rates of income taxation, inflation pushes taxpayers into higher tax rate brackets, even though the taxpayer purchasing power may not have increased – or may have actually gone down. So inflation acts as an automatic and invisible

Finance Made Easy (2nd Edition)

tax rate increase – which can be most convenient for government. Government can benefit by this beneficial plum simply falling right into their lap, while making no apparent effort to raise taxes.

Another inflation incentive for government is that inflation automatically lightens the burden of government debt. The valuable dollars borrowed by the government are repaid in dollars of lesser purchasing power. In effect, the government borrows big dollars and repays its debts in small dollars. Again, this beneficial plum simply falls right into the lap of government, while the government makes no apparent effort to repay its debts in a debased currency. So there is another incentive for government to inflate the currency. In effect, inflation rewards debtors who owe money, and hurts creditors, to whom money is owed.

Given these government incentives that favor inflation, it is not surprising that inflation is quite common, and far from rare.

Therefore the risk-free rate of return must include an amount to:

1. Compensate for delaying consumption;
2. Compensate for inflation.

Now we ask: why is the rate of return on the entire market greater than the risk-free rate of return? The difference is because the rate of return on the entire market includes an allowance for risk, but by definition, the risk-free rate of return excludes an allowance for risk. Therefore all rates of return (and all rates of interest) include an amount to compensate for:

1. Delaying consumption;
2. Inflation;
3. Risk.

Only the risk-free rate of return does not include an allowance for risk. But all other rates of return (and rates of interest) must include allowances for delaying consumption, expected inflation, and risk.

These are important concepts, and they should be borne in mind throughout the chapters to follow.

Chapter Summary

This chapter dealt with the following key topics:

1. Risk and reward;
2. High and low risk compared with high and low reward;
3. Measuring risk;
4. Using the standard deviation;
5. Risk versus uncertainty;
6. Risk reduction;
7. Compensating for risk by raising the required rate of return;
8. The Capital Asset Pricing Model (CAPM);
9. The three components of rates of return;

Practice Problems

1. How are risk and reward connected?
   Answer: generally it is said that
   increased risk is compensated by
   increased reward, so that risk and
   reward go hand in hand. But more
   precisely, increased risk is
   compensated by the probability of
   increased reward, accompanied by the
   probability of increased penalty.
   However, along with increased risk is
   the decreased probability of large
   rewards or penalties. So while the
   rewards and penalties of increased
   risk might grow in magnitude, the
   probability of actually obtaining these
   increased rewards and penalties may
   shrink.

2. How can risk be measured? Answer:
   when there are available data of
   regular and recurring variables, the
   standard deviation may be used as an
   indicator of risk.

25

3. Does risk differ from uncertainty, and, if so, how? Answer: under risk there are available data of regular and recurring variables, and the standard deviation may be used as an indicator of risk. In the absence of available data of regular and recurring variables, there is uncertainty, and there is no standard deviation to be used as an indicator of risk.

4. How do organizations use strategies to reduce risk, and what are some of these strategies? Answer: some strategies are reducing the volatility of sales and spreading of fixed costs by means of market segmentation (discounts for select groups but not for all), insuring against various disasters or legal liabilities, and diversification of activities or geographical location.

5. How do organizations compensate for risk? Answer: one method is to increase the required rate of return for various projects according to the

estimated amount of risk. For example, a routine replacement of used machinery by similar equipment might be done at a moderate required rate of return, but introducing a radical new product to a new market may demand a much higher required rate of return.

6. What are the components of rates of return other than the risk-free rate of return? Answer: all rates of return other than the risk-free rate of return include three components to compensate for delay of consumption, expected inflation, and risk.

Chapter 2

Time Is Money

If you would know the value of money,
go and try to borrow some.

Benjamin Franklin

The Time Value Of Money

Would you rather have $100 right now, or
$100 a year from now? If you had $100
right now, you could invest it and have more
than $100 a year from now. So the right
answer is right now, rather than a year from
now. For example, if a safe investment paid
interest of 3% per year, your $100 would
amount to $103 a year from now. Therefore
$100 right now is worth $103 a year from
now.   That is why the value of money

28

Finance Made Easy (2nd Edition)

depends on time. And that is why finance is based on the time value of money.

Time may be present or future. Likewise, the value of money may be expressed as present or future. As we have seen, the present value of $100 is $100. But the future value of $100 at a safe interest rate of 3% per year is $103. By the same token, the present value of $100 a year from now at a safe interest rate of 3% per year is $100/1.03 = $97.09. Check it out by reversing our calculation: the future value of $97.09 at a safe interest rate of 3% per year is $97.09 x 1.03 = $100.

What we have established to this point is that money has a time value, so that its present value is different from its future value. But we have only considered now versus a year from now. What about 2 years from now? For example, what if we invest $100 now for 2 years at a safe interest rate of 3% per year? We already know that we will have $103 a year from now. By the end of year 2, will we earn another $3 in interest? That would make our future value in 2 years $103 + $3 = $106. Or will the year 2 interest be 3% of $103, which is $103 x 1.03 = $106.09?

Simple and Compound Interest

This difference of 9 cents between $106 and $106.09 may seem trivial. But in actual fact it is far from trivial. For example, over 20 years at $3 interest per year we will earn total interest of 20 x $3 = $60. Added to our original $100 that gives us $160. But using the alternate approach, we end up with $100 x 1.03 x 1.03 x 1.03 ... or $100(1.03)^{20} = $180.61. Now there is an appreciable difference between $160 and $180.61. Therefore over time this small difference adds up, and is far from trivial.

What we have come across is simple interest (the $3 each year) versus compound interest (which is $100 x 1.03 x 1.03 x 1.03 ...) and which amounts to earning interest on interest.

So simple interest is interest earned only upon the principal ($100 in our example). But compound interest is interest earned on both principal and interest. This is an important difference to keep in mind. In finance we should always be aware of the difference between simple and compound interest. If this difference is not made explicit, one should automatically assume that compound interest applies. In other words, compound interest is the default position.

Finding The Time Value of Money

We have already explored present value and future value, for a single period and for multiple periods. What else may we need to know about the time value of money? Consider this question: Tiffany needs a new car. She can afford to pay $350 per month and needs an auto loan of $15,000. She can finance $15,000 at interest of 1% per month. How many months will it take to pay off her auto loan in full? This question asks us how many periods it takes.

Another question about the time value of money might relate to the rate of interest involved. For example: Tiffany needs a new car. She can afford to

pay $350 per month and needs an auto loan of $15,000. If she wants to have her auto loan fully paid off in 60 months, what rate of interest can she afford to pay on the loan?

Another question about the time value of money might ask: Tiffany needs a new car. She can obtain an auto loan of $15,000. She wants to have her auto loan fully paid off in 60 months, and the monthly rate of interest is 1%. How much can she afford to pay monthly on the loan?

The questions about the time value of money can be summarized this way. There are 5 variables as follows:

1. Present Value (PV)

2. Future Value (FV)

3. Number of Periods (NPER)

4. Rate of Return[2] (RATE)

5. Regular Periodic Payment (PMT)

Notice that there are 5 variables regarding the time value of money. Given any 4 variables, we can always find the one remaining unknown variable. There are several different methods to find the one unknown variable. We can use algebra, or a financial calculator, or a computer. By far the easiest method is to use the computer and a software program like Microsoft Excel[3]. Excel has financial functions, where one can insert the amount of each known

---

[2] Or rate of interest.
[3] Alternatively, there are other suitable software programs like Open Office, which is freeware.

variable, and the financial function will then automatically provide the one unknown variable. Excel is the best number-cruncher on the planet, and is used by financial professionals throughout the world. That is why Excel is recommended by this book for all time value of money calculations.

Free Excel Tutorials Online

If you are not familiar with Excel and the Excel financial functions, here are some free tutorials on the internet:

1) http://office.microsoft.com/en-us/excel-help/plan-payments-and-savings-in-excel-2010-RZ102630204.aspx
2) http://www.homeandlearn.co.uk/excel2007/excel2007s5p5.html
3) http://www.learnmicrosoftexcel.com/free_tutorials/free_tutorials_with_video.htm
4) There are many other free internet tutorials on Excel and the Excel

financial functions. Just do a Google search for "free internet tutorials on Excel" in order to obtain access.

Examples of Time Value of Money Calculations

Let us go back to the example of Tiffany and her car for sample calculations of the time value of money. Recall that Tiffany needs a new car. She can obtain an auto loan of $15,000. She wants to have her auto loan fully paid off in 60 months, and the monthly rate of interest is 1%. Tiffany can afford to make monthly payments of $350 on her auto loan. For practice, use Excel to calculate the following items, and use the answers provided to check your results:

1) What is the present value of Tiffany's first payment, made at the end of month one? Using the Excel present value function (PV), enter the following data:

Finance Made Easy (2nd Edition)

RATE	0.01
NPER	1
PMT	- 350
FV	

The answer is $346.53. Note the minus sign next to PMT -350. The PMT is a cash outflow. There must be a minus sign next to all cash outflows. Also note that the FV category is left blank, because there is no future value – this is paying off a loan, not accumulating a future sum. Note that we have calculated present value for just one single period. Next, we use the Excel present value function (PV) for multiple periods.

2) What is the present value of Tiffany's total stream of payments, made at the end of every month for all 60 months? Using the Excel present value function (PV), enter the following data:

RATE	0.01
NPER	60
PMT	-350

This present value for all 60 periods amounts to $15,734.26 – which is roughly close to Tiffany's loan of $15,000. Tiffany's total loan payments are 60 x $350, which add up to $21,000. She borrowed $15,734.26, which means her loan interest amounts to $21,000 - $15,734.26 = $5,265.74 over 60 months.

3) What is the future value of Tiffany's total stream of payments, made at the end of every month for all 60 months? Using the Excel future value function (FV), enter the following data:

RATE	0.01
NPER	60
PMT	-350

This future value for all 60 periods amounts to $28,584.38. In other words, 60 monthly installments of $350 each, at interest of 1% per month will amount to $28,584.38.

4) How many periods are required for Tiffany to pay off an auto loan at 1% interest per month if the monthly installment is $350? Using the Excel number of periods function (NPER), enter the following data:

RATE	0.01
PMT	-350
PV	15734.26

The answer to the NPER function is 60 – which we know is the correct number of months.

5) What rate of interest per month is Tiffany paying on her auto loan of $15,734.26 with 60 monthly payments of $350 each?

Using the Excel RATE function, enter the following data:

NPER	60
PMT	-350
PV	15734.26

The answer to the RATE calculation in Excel is 1%, which we know to be the correct rate of interest per month.

6) Finally, we compute how much Tiffany must pay each month on her auto loan of $15,734.26 with 60 monthly payments at 1% interest per month. We use the Excel payment (PMT) function, and enter the following data:

RATE	0.01
NPER	60
PV	15734.26

The answer to the Excel PMT function is $350, which we know to be the correct loan repayment installment per month.

We have demonstrated the basic time value of money calculations using Excel financial functions.

The Compounding Period

Interest may be compounded annually, quarterly, monthly, weekly, daily, or even continuously. It is important to be consistent when solving time value of money problems. For example, Dawn is getting a 30-year mortgage loan. She is borrowing $250,000 at 4.75% per annum. How much is her monthly payment?

Note the inconsistency between the interest rate at 4.75% per annum and calculation of her monthly payment. We need to convert the interest rate and the mortgage period from an annual to a monthly basis, as follows. Using the Excel PMT function, we have:

RATE	0.0475/12
NPER	30*12
PV	250000

Note that the interest rate and the periodic payment are on a consistent monthly basis. The answer is a monthly payment of $1,304.12. Check it out.

Beginning or Ending Cash Flows

So far, we have implicitly assumed that all cash flows occur at the end of each period. In fact, that is the normal default assumption in Excel. So, if all cash flows occur at the end of each period, just do nothing. But, if it so happens that cash flows take place at the beginning of each period, rather than the end of each period, then simply insert a "1" in the last section of the Excel function variable input list.

The Rule of 72

Here is a handy rule of thumb that provides a useful mental approximation. It is known as the "Rule of 72." For example, at 6% interest per annum, how many years will it take for money to double? The answer is 72/6 = 12 years. At 9% interest per annum, how many years will it take for money to double? The answer is 72/9 = 8 years. At 12% interest per annum, how many years will it take for money to double? The answer is 72/12 = 6 years. The Rule of 72 approximates how many periods it will take for money to double by dividing 72 by the periodic rate of interest. The Rule of 72 can also approximate the periodic rate of interest. For example, at what periodic rate of interest will money double in 30 months? The answer is 72/30 = 2.4% per month. Bear in mind that these answers are approximations rather than precise amounts. The approximations are fairly good, but not exact.

Perpetuities

A perpetuity is a regular periodic payment continuing forever. For example, there is a British government bond known as a Consol. Consols carry a fixed rate of interest, but never mature. So there is continuing periodic payment of interest, but never a payment of principal. How are perpetuities valued? Simply divide the periodic payment on the perpetuity by the rate of return. For example, a perpetuity pays $30 per year. At a 10% rate of return, what is it worth? Answer: $30/10% = $300. Why is this correct? Because the return of $30 per year is 10% of the $300 cost of the perpetuity.

Chapter Summary

In summary, there are there are 5 variables regarding the time value of money. These variables are as follows:

1) Present Value

2) Future Value
3) Number of Periods
4) Rate of Interest
5) Periodic Payment

Given any 4 variables, we can always find the one unknown variable. This is easily done by using the Excel financial functions, which are as follows:

1) PV
2) FV
3) NPER
4) RATE
5) PMT

These basic financial functions are the foundation of finance, and will be used throughout this book, as we further explain and illustrate the techniques of financial management.

Further, we explained that there needs to be consistency between time periods when solving time value of money problems.

Finally, we illustrated a useful approximation, known as the "Rule of 72."

Practice Problems

Here are practice problems, together with the answers, for you to use in order to help you become familiar with the basic Excel financial functions. Stuart Brown has just won a lottery prize of $85,000 a year for 10 years. He asks you the following questions:

1) At an interest rate of 5% per year, what is the present value of his lottery prize of $85,000 a year for 10 years? Answer: $656,347.47.

2) At an interest rate of 5% per year, what is the future value of his lottery prize of $85,000 a year for 10 years? Answer: $1,069,120.87

3) Stuart wants to accumulate $1,069,120.87 and can invest $85,000 at the end of each year on which he earns 5% interest every year. How

many years will this take? Answer: 10 years.

4) Stuart wants to accumulate $1,069,120.87 and can invest $85,000 at the end of each year. To accomplish this, what annual rate of interest must he earn? Answer: 5%.

5) Stuart wants to accumulate $1,069,120.87 in 10 years from now. At 5% interest, how much must he invest at the end of each year? Answer: $85,000.

Chapter 3

Cost of Capital

Capital is that part of wealth which is devoted to obtaining further wealth.

Alfred Marshall

Capital Structure

There is a distinction between working capital and long-term capital structure. Working capital tends to be short-term, while capital structure tends to be long-term. Consider a typical balance sheet:

Assets	**Liabilities&Equity**
Current Assets	Current Liabilities
Noncurrent Assets	*Long-Term Liabilities*
	Preferred Stock
	Common Equity
Total Assets	Total Liabilities & Equity

Working capital is Current Assets less Current Liabilities, and is generally used to maintain current liquidity. In other words, Current Assets such as inventory, accounts receivable, and cash, tend to be financed by Current Liabilities. On the other hand, Noncurrent Assets, such as Land, Buildings, Plant and Equipment, tend to be financed by the long-term capital structure, which consists of Long-Term Liabilities, Preferred Stock, and Common Equity. And when we refer to the "cost of capital" we mean the cost of the long-term capital structure.

Long-Term Liabilities

Long-Term liabilities consist mainly of long-term debt. Long-term debt for private companies usually represents long-term borrowing to acquire Noncurrent Assets, such as Land, Buildings, Plant and Equipment. For public companies long-term debt is often represented by Bonds Payable. Bonds are usually sold to the public, and the bondholders may either resell their bonds, or hold them until maturity, when they will be repaid in full.

Bonds are usually issued in units of $1,000 each, and tend to have a fixed rate of interest and a maturity of 20 years – although maturities can be shorter or longer than 20 years. Bond interest is usually paid every 6 months to registered bondholders. Bond principal is usually repaid in full at maturity. Bonds are usually described as ABC Company 7% bonds of 2040 – which indicates that the bond issuer is ABC

Company, the rate of interest is 7% per year, and the bonds mature in the year 2040.

Some bonds are mortgage bonds (secured by land and buildings), and some bonds are unsecured. In bankruptcy, interest and principal on secured bonds must be repaid in full before any repayment of interest or principal on unsecured bonds. And interest and principal on unsecured bonds must be repaid in full before anything can be paid on preferred or common stock.

Preferred Stock

Preferred stock is junior to bonds, but senior to common stock. Preferred stock may be redeemable (repaid at maturity, like a bond) or not redeemable (without a date of maturity, meaning no repayment at any time). Whether or not redeemable, preferred stock carries a fixed rate of dividend. For example, preferred stock is usually described as DEF Company 6% redeemable preferred (if it is redeemable) or simply DEF

Company 6% preferred (if it is not redeemable) – which indicates that the preferred issuer is DEF Company, and the rate of dividend is 6% per year. In addition, the preferred stock might or might not be cumulative. Cumulative preferred has a cumulative dividend, which means that any missed preferred dividends must be paid in full before any dividend at all can be paid on common stock. If the preferred stock is not cumulative, then missed preferred dividends do not have to be made up. However, no dividend can be paid on common stock until the current dividend on preferred has been paid in full.

Common Equity

The common equity consists of the proceeds from the sale of common stock, plus any stock premium (stock premium is any money obtained by selling common stock in excess of its par value), plus Retained Earnings (which are earnings remaining undistributed by way of dividends).

Common equity is junior to preferred stock, which in turn is junior to bonds payable. Therefore common equity is the most junior of all securities.

Cost of Capital

In general, return is directly related to risk. The greater the risk involved, the greater is the return required by investors. It follows that the less the risk involved, the less is the return required by investors. Risk is shown by the degree to which securities are junior or senior to other securities. In general, common equity carries the most risk because it is the most junior of all securities. Therefore common equity is highest in risk, and highest in the return required by investors.

Preferred stock is intermediate in risk and return, compared with common equity, on the one hand, and bonds, on the other hand. Bonds are the most senior securities, carrying the least risk as well as the lowest return.

Leverage

Corporations face some trade-offs when it comes to capital structure. On the one hand, the cost of bonds is lower than the cost of preferred stock or common equity, because bonds are the most senior securities, carrying the least risk as well as the lowest return. Further, the interest expense of bonds is tax-deductible, whereas dividends paid on preferred and common stocks are not tax-deductible. So there are very attractive reasons for corporations to maximize the proportion of bonds in their capital structure.

On the other hand, there is also a very good reason for corporations not to maximize the proportion of bonds in their capital structure. Interest on bonds must be paid regardless of whether times are good or bad. Interest on bonds must be paid regardless of whether profits are high, low, or even non-existent. If a corporation is making losses, rather than profits, it must still pay the interest on its bonds. In other words, there are compelling reasons for corporations to maximize the proportion of bonds in their capital structure. There are also compelling reasons for corporations to minimize the proportion of bonds in their capital structure.

The proportion of bonds in the capital structure is known as leverage. The greater the proportion of bonds in the capital structure, the greater the leverage. And the greater the leverage, the higher is the risk. Leverage has been compared to alcohol in that it makes the good times better, but the bad times worse.

The Cost of Capital – an Example

Imagine that XYZ Corporation has the following capital structure:

Capital Structure	Amount ($'000)	Percentage
5% Bonds	35,000	35%
7% Preferred Stock	10,000	10%
Common Equity	55,000	55%
Total Capital Structure	100,000	100%

In addition, XYZ Corporation has a tax rate of 30% and a cost of equity of 12%. The XYZ Corporation has the following weighted average cost of capital (WACC).

WACC	Percentage	Cost	Weighted Cost
Bonds	35%	3.5%[4]	1.225%
Preferred	10%	7.0%	0.700%
Common	55%	12.0%	6.600%
Total	**100%**		**8.525%**

The WACC is 8.525%. We use the weighted average cost of capital because it is not practicable to tell whether any particular dollar of long-term capital came from debt or preferred stock or common equity. Therefore we recognize that long-term capital consists of a blend of long-term debt, preferred and common equity. Accordingly, we regard the cost of long-term capital as the weighted average cost of capital.

Flotation Cost

It takes money to issue bonds. Those bond issue costs are known as "flotation costs." In

---

[4] The after-tax interest rate is 5% times (1- tax rate) = 5% x (1-30%) = 5% x 70% = 3.5%

order to allow for flotation costs the cost of long-term debt must take flotation costs into account. So the cost of long-term debt is:

Total Annual Interest Expense(1-t)/(Bond Sale Receipts-Flotation Costs)

For example, FGH Corporation issues $100 million of 8% bonds. Flotation costs are $200,000 and the tax rate is 35%. The cost of these bonds, using the above formula is as follows:

$8,000,000(1-0.35)/($100,000,000-$200,000) = 5.21%

Please note that flotation costs should also be taken into account for preferred stock and common stock.

Yield to Maturity

Consider again the example where FGH Corporation issues $100 million of 8% bonds. The par value of each bond is $1,000, and the bonds are to be redeemed after 20 years at a premium of $100 to par (namely $1,100). After the bonds are issued, they trade at $1,200 each. The buyer of one 8% bond is buying the right to receive cash flows of $80 each year for 20 years, plus $1,100 at the end of 20 years. The cash flows of $80 each year are actually received as $40 every 6 months. What average annual interest rate is earned on this bond from now until maturity?

In order to answer this question we use the Excel RATE function as follows:

NPER	20*2
PMT	80/2
PV	-1200
FV	1100

The answer is 3.23%. Of course, the 3.23% is received every 6 months. This 3.23% needs to be multiplied by 2 to state it on an annual basis. So the annual yield to maturity is 2 x 3.23% = 6.46%.

Bond Values

In the above example of FGH Corporation 8% bonds we are told that after the bonds are issued, they trade at $1,200 each. Why would an 8% bond trade at $1,200? The reason is that the going rate of interest on bonds like the FGH Corporation 8% bonds is less than 8%. Since this bond pays more than the going rate of interest on similar bonds it trades at a premium. As we have seen, the yield to maturity on this bond is 6.46% per annum. Therefore the going rate is 6.46% per annum. Given that this bond pays more than the going rate of interest, it trades at a premium.   By the same token, bonds that pay less than the going rate of interest will trade at a discount.

We have learned that bonds trade at a premium or a discount. The amount of premium or discount depends on whether the bond in question pays interest at a rate above or below the going rate of interest on similar bonds. Bonds paying more than the going rate of interest on similar bonds will trade at a premium. Bonds paying less than the going rate of interest on similar bonds will trade at a discount.

Having learned that, what will happen to bond prices if the going rate of interest decreases? The bond prices will increase. And what will happen to bond prices if the going rate of interest increases? The bond prices will decrease. This principle is very important. Therefore we will show it below in the form of a table.

	Bond Price
Going Rate of Interest Decrease	*Increases*
Going Rate of Interest Increase	*Decreases*

A good way to remember this important principle is that bond prices move in the opposite direction to changes in the going rate of interest. Incidentally, the going rate of interest is sometimes referred to as the market rate of interest. And bear in mind that there are many different rates of interest, not just one rate of interest. Rates of return vary according to degrees of risk. So there are as many rates of interest as there are shades of risk.

The Cost of Preferred Stock

The cost of preferred stock is calculated in the same manner as a bond. But there is no tax deduction for payment of a preferred dividend. So no tax adjustment is necessary for a preferred stock. Therefore the cost of preferred stock is simply the annual preferred dividend per share divided by the current price of the preferred stock net of the flotation cost per preferred share. For example, IJK Corporation issues a preferred stock paying an annual dividend of $6 per preferred share, and incurs a flotation cost of $2 per preferred share. The preferred stock is trading at $90 per share. The cost of preferred stock is $6/($90-$2) = 6.8%.

The Cost of Common Stock

The cost of common stock is more difficult to measure than the cost of preferred stock because common stock does not have a fixed rate of dividend like preferred stock. There are three approaches to estimating the cost of common stock.

The Dividend Approach, also known as the Gordon Model. This approach recognizes that dividends are the only cash flows paid by the corporation to its common stockholders. The present value (P_0) of common stock is the next period dividend (D_1) divided by the required rate of return (k) per period on this stock less the expected growth rate of the dividend (g). The present value of this stream of future dividends is as follows:

$$P_0 = D_1/(k\text{-}g)$$

Rearranging this equation to derive k, the cost of common stock, we get:

$$k = D_1/ P_0 + g$$

For example, imagine that LMO Corporation common stock is trading at $55 per share. Next year's common stock dividend is expected to be $4.80 and is expected to grow indefinitely at 4% per year.

$k = \$4.80/\$55 + 0.04 = 0.1273 = 12.73\%$ The

CAPM Approach is the Capital Asset Pricing Model (CAPM). The CAPM formula for cost of common stock is as follows:

$$k = RF + (M\text{-}RF)\beta$$

where RF is the risk-free rate of interest (on government bonds), M is the expected rate of return on the entire stock market, and β the beta of the company's common stock (which is a measure of the risk of the company's stock, relative to the risk of the entire universe of stocks (standardized as 1.0). The term (M-RF) is also known as the "risk premium" because it represents the premium of the return on the entire stock market (which involves risk) over the risk-free rate of interest (on government bonds, which are regarded as no risk, because as a last resort the government can raise funds by taxation, if all else fails).

For example, assume that PQR Corporation common stock has a beta of 1.2, the risk-free rate of interest is 2.5% and the expected rate of return on the entire market is 10%. Then:

$$k = 2.5\% + (10\%-2.5\%)1.2 = (10\%)1.2 = 12.0\%$$

The Risk Premium Approach

The risk premium approach adds the "risk premium" (M-RF) to the company's cost of debt in order to estimate the cost of common stock. In the example above, the risk premium was 7.5%. Assume that the after-tax cost of debt is 4.9%. Then the risk premium approach would add 7.5% to 4.9% giving a total of 12.4% as the estimate the cost of common stock.

Comparison of All Three Methods of Estimating the Cost of Common Stock

All three methods above of estimating the cost of common stock can be summarized as follows:

MethodofEstimation	Result
Dividend Approach	12.73%
CAPM Approach	12.0%
Risk Premium Approach	12.4%

The Cost of Common Equity

The cost of common stock does not tell us the cost of retained earnings. Retained earnings are undistributed profits that are reinvested in the business by common stockholders. That makes retained earnings akin to the funds originally invested in the business by common stockholders.

Therefore retained earnings are tantamount to common stock, and have the same cost as common stock. As a matter of fact, all components of common equity are tantamount to common stock, and have the same cost as common stock. Therefore the cost of common equity and the cost of common stock are one and the same.

Cumulative or Incremental Cost of Capital

Much of the time capital investment projects are funded by existing financial resources In that case, the cost of capital is based on the existing capital structure – in other words, we use the cumulative cost of capital. But on occasion a few capital investment projects are funded by specially issued securities. So when this is the case, the cost of capital for that specific project will be the cost of the particular securities issued to fund that specific project.

Chapter Summary

This chapter covered the following topics:

1. Capital structure
2. Leverage
3. The cost of long-term debt
4. The cost of preferred stock
5. The cost of common equity
6. The weighted average cost of capital

Practice Problems

The following practice problems are provided, together with answers so that you can check whether your results are correct.

1. What is the difference (if any) between working capital and the capital structure? Answer: working capital is short-term funding to support current assets such as inventory, accounts receivable, and cash. Capital structure is long-term debt, preferred stock, and common equity for financing long-term assets such as land, buildings, plant, machinery, and equipment.

2. Can we tell which sources of funds were used to acquire specific long-term assets? For example, was the new milling machine bought with debt or preferred stock or common stock or retained earnings? If so, how can we tell? If not, what do we do about it? Answer: we cannot tell which sources of funds were used to acquire specific assets. Instead we recognize that all long-term assets were acquired by using a blend of debt, preferred stock, and common equity, in the same proportions of debt, preferred stock and common equity in the total capital structure. To represent the cost of

Finance Made Easy (2nd Edition)
this blend of funds, we use the weighted average cost of capital.

3. Minerva Corporation has the following capital structure: $750 million of 6.5% bonds, issued with flotation costs of $10 million. No preferred stock, but $1 billion of common stock, issued with flotation costs of $20 million. Retained earnings are $250 million, and the firm has a tax rate of 30%. Next year's dividend is expected to be $100 million and to grow at 5% per year. What is the WACC of Minerva Corporation? Answer: the after tax cost of debt is [(6.5% of $750 million)/ ($750 million - $10 million)](1-t) = [(48.75)/(740)]0.7 = 0.0461 = 4.61%. The cost of common equity, using the dividend approach formula is $k = D_1/ P_0 + g$ = 100/(980+250) + 0.05 = 0.1313 = 13.13%.

Finance Made Easy (2nd Edition)

Capital Structure	Amount	%	Cost	WACC
Debt	750	37.5%	4.61%	1.73%
Common Equity	1,250	62.5%	13.13%	8.21%
WACC		100.0%		10.04%

4. Minerva Corporation 6.5% bonds were issued at a discount of $100 and mature at a premium of $100 in 10 years. They pay interest every 6 months. What is their yield to maturity? Answer: using the Excel RATE function we have 4.33% x 2 = 8.66% per annum based on the inputs below.

NPER	10*2
PMT	65/2
PV	1000-100
FV	1000+100

5. Minerva Corporation common stock has a beta of 1.6. The risk free rate is 2.5% and the return on the entire market of common stocks is 9%. What is the cost of Minerva common equity? Answer:

using the CAPM formula, we have k = RF + (M-RF)β = 2.5% + (9%-2.5%)1.6 = 12.9%.

6. Using the risk premium approach, what is the cost of Minerva common equity? Answer: The risk premium approach formula is the cost of Minerva debt (4.61%) plus the risk premium (M-RF = 9%-2.5% = 6.5%) = 4.61% + 6.5% = 11.11%.

7. What is leverage and what are its advantages and disadvantages? Answer: The proportion of long-term debt in the capital structure is known as leverage. The greater the proportion of long-term debt in the capital structure, the greater the leverage. And the greater the leverage, the higher the risk. On the one hand, the cost of long-term debt is lower than the cost of preferred stock or common equity, because long-term debt is the most senior security, carrying the least risk as well as the lowest return. Further, the interest

expense of long-term debt is tax-deductible, whereas dividends paid on preferred and common stocks are not tax-deductible. So there are very attractive reasons for corporations to maximize the proportion of long-term debt in their capital structure.

On the other hand, there is also a very good reason for corporations not to maximize the proportion of bonds in their capital structure. Interest on long-term debt must be paid regardless of whether times are good or bad. Interest on long-term debt must be paid regardless of whether profits are high, low, or even non-existent. If a corporation is making losses, rather than profits, it must still pay the interest on its long-term debt.

In other words, there are compelling reasons for corporations to maximize the proportion of long-term debt in their capital structure. There are also compelling reasons for corporations to minimize the proportion of long-term debt in their capital structure. Leverage has been compared to alcohol in that it makes the good times better, but the bad times worse.

Chapter 4

Required Rate of Return

It's true hard work never killed anybody, but I figure, why take the chance?

Ronald Reagan

Is WACC the Required Rate of Return?

In Chapter 3 we learned about the weighted average cost of capital (WACC). Capital has a cost, and therefore when capital is invested, it must earn enough to cover its cost. Does that mean that WACC is the rate of return that capital investments must earn in order to cover the cost of invested capital? That may seem logical, but the correct answer is not that simple.

First, there are a few capital investment projects that earn no return at all. For instance, complying with environmental laws can require installation of pollution control equipment, which may be costly, but which earns no return. Another example is the purchase and installation of safety equipment that protects workers from injury. Safety equipment may be costly, but – like pollution control equipment - safety equipment also earns no return.

So, the capital investment projects that do earn a return have to earn a return large enough to cover their own cost of capital as well as the cost of capital for capital investment projects that earn no return at all.

For example, imagine the WACC for Ajax Corporation is 9%, but one-tenth of Ajax Corporation capital investment projects earn no return at all. Those capital investment projects earn no return because they are pollution controls and safety equipment. In order to compensate for the lack of returns on those capital investment projects, the remaining capital investment projects must earn an extra amount, over and above their own cost of capital.

So instead of earning the WACC of 9%, the remaining capital investment projects must earn 10% in order to cover the cost of capital for the pollution controls and safety equipment, which do not earn a rate of return. In other words, the capital investment projects that do earn a return must earn an additional return in order to pay for capital investment projects that earn no return. That is one adjustment to WACC that must be made. Other adjustments to WACC must also be made in order to take risk into account.

WACC Adjustments for Risk

Capital investment projects may differ considerably with respect to risk. For example imagine that Ajax Corporation is researching a new approach to a cure for cancer. This new approach is not a drug or a machine or a chemical substance. Rather it is a rare mineral mined in only one remote region in the world. This potential cure for cancer will need to first be developed from a small supply of the rare mineral in the laboratory, then it will undergo a series of tests on animals of various species.

If these animal tests are successful, the potential cure for cancer will undergo a series of tests on human beings. If these human tests are successful, then the potential cure for cancer will need to be tested again on humans against a placebo. Only if the potential cure for cancer shows that it is effective compared to placebo[5] will Ajax Corporation be allowed to patent and to market the potential cure for cancer. Therefore this project is likely to take many years to complete, and its cost is likely to be extremely high. It is vastly more risky than a routine capital investment by Ajax Corporation such as replacing a fleet of trucks.

Given that capital investment projects may differ considerably with respect to risk, most large corporations develop categories of capital investment project risk. Here is an example of categories of capital investment project risk.:

---

[55] To be proven effective compared to placebo, the potential cure for cancer must be statistically significant versus placebo in a controlled double blind experiment that is of adequate design and of satisfactory sample sizes.

Project Type	Risk
Routine replacements	Minimal
Cost Reduction	Low
Expand Existing Products in Existing Markets	Moderate
Add New Products in Existing Markets	Moderate-High
Expand Existing Products into New Markets	Moderate-High
New Products in New Markets	High

Therefore, when setting the required rate of return for the acceptance of various capital investment projects, the required rate of return must be set by taking into account the following items:

Start with	WACC
Add allowance for capital investment projects with no returns, such as pollution controls or safety equipment	+ no return adjustment
Add allowance for capital investment project risk, based upon the project risk category and tailored to fit each individual capital investment project's risk characteristics	+ individual risk adjustment
End up with hurdle rate for each specific project	Sum of the above

Here is an example: Ajax Corporation has a WACC of 9.3%. About 12% of its capital investment projects have no cash inflows because they are for pollution reduction and safety equipment. The Capital investment Committee is presently reviewing a proposed capital investment project to buy new production machines that are estimated to reduce annual production costs by a significant amount. What hurdle rate should the proposed cost saving project have to meet? Answer:

WACC	9.3%
Adjustment for projects with no cash inflows: 9.3% times 100/88	10.57%
Add allowance for project risk (low)	1.0%
Hurdle rate for cost saving project	11.57%

Here is another example: the Ajax Corporation information about the WACC and the capital investment projects have no cash inflows remains unchanged. But now the Capital investment Committee is reviewing a proposed capital investment project to enter a new market with a new product which has just been developed.

Finance Made Easy (2nd Edition)

What hurdle rate should the proposed new product project have to meet? Answer:

WACC	9.3%
Adjustment for projects with no cash inflows: 9.3% times 100/88	10.57%
Add allowance for project risk (high)	8.0%
Hurdle rate for cost saving project	18.57%

Note that the hurdle rate for the proposed new product project is much higher than the hurdle rate of 11.57% for the proposed cost saving project. The addition to the hurdle rate is made necessary by the much more risky nature of the proposed new product project compared to the relatively low risk of the proposed cost saving project.

Chapter Summary

1. Is WACC the Required Rate of Return?

2. No – the WACC should be increased to cover the cost of capital for capital investment projects which have no cash inflows.
3. In addition, the WACC should be increased to cover the extent of the risk that is estimated for each individual capital investment project.

Practice Problems

1. The Ajax Corporation information about the WACC and the capital investment projects have no cash inflows remains unchanged. But now the Capital investment Committee is reviewing a proposed capital investment project to expand an existing product in an existing market.

    Answer:

WACC	9.3%
Adjustment for projects with no cash inflows: 9.3% times 100/88	10.57%
Add allowance for project risk (low)	1.00%
Hurdle rate for cost saving project	11.57%

2. The Ajax Corporation information about the WACC and the capital investment projects have no cash inflows remains unchanged. But now the Capital investment Committee is reviewing a proposed capital investment project to expand an existing product in an existing market. Answer:

WACC	9.3%
Adjustment for projects with no cash inflows: 9.3% times 100/88	10.57%
Add allowance for project risk (moderate)	2.50%
Hurdle rate for cost saving project	13.07%

3. The Ajax Corporation information about the WACC and the capital investment projects have no cash inflows remains unchanged. But now the Capital investment Committee is reviewing a proposed capital investment project to expand an existing product in a new market. Answer:

WACC	9.3%
Adjustment for projects with no cash inflows: 9.3% times 100/88	10.57%
Add allowance for project risk (moderate-high)	6.00%
Hurdle rate for cost saving project	16.57%

Chapter 5

Capital Budgeting

Every day I get up and look through the Forbes list of the richest people in America. If I'm not there, I go to work.

Robert Orben?

What is Capital Budgeting?

Managers often have several capital investment projects competing for a limited amount of available funds with which to finance the projects. How can they select which capital investment projects to fund, and which to reject, or defer? This process of selecting which capital investment projects to fund is known as capital budgeting. One approach to this issue is to use the payback method.

The Payback Method

The payback method prioritizes capital investment projects according to how quickly they pay for themselves. More precisely, the payback method favors those projects that repay their initial investment in the fewest number of time periods. For example:

Capital Project	Initial Investment ($million)	Annual Cash Inflow ($million)	Payback In # of Years
A	13	3	4.3
B	5	1	5.0
C	17	12	1.4

The fastest payback is from project C = 1.4 years.

The main advantage of the payback method is its simplicity. It is quick and easy to use. But it has two huge faults, as follows:

1. It does not look beyond the payback year. So project C above may only have cash inflows for 2 years, while project A may have cash inflows for 25 years.
2. It does not take into account the time value of money.

These two huge faults limit the usefulness of the payback method, and render it unsuitable for selecting which capital investment projects to fund.

The Present Value Method

In order to avoid the faults of the payback method, we can turn to a method we have already used: the present value method.

To apply the present value method, we need the following information:
1. The hurdle rate for each project.
2. The timing and amount of the cash inflows and outflows for each project.

For instance, let us re-use our recent example, with a different last column:

Capital Project	Initial Investment ($million)	Annual Cash Inflow ($ million)	For This Many Years
A	13	3	25
B	5	1	9
C	17	12	2

Using a hurdle rate of 12% and the Excel PV function, we find the present value of each project's cash inflows as follows:

Capital Project	Initial Investment ($million)	PV of Cash Inflows ($million)
A	13	23.53
B	5	5.33
C	17	20.28

Having found the present value of the cash inflows, our last step is to deduct the initial investment from the present value of each project's cash inflows, as follows:

Capital Project	Initial Investment ($million)	PV of Cash Inflows ($ million)	Net PV Of Cash Flows ($ million)
A	13	23.53	10.53
B	5	5.33	0.33
C	17	20.28	3.28

We see that the three capital investment projects can now be ranked in their order of merit, as follows:

Capital Project	Initial Investment ($million)	PV of Cash Inflows ($ million)	Net PV Of Cash Flows ($ million)
A	13	23.53	10.53
C	17	20.28	3.28
B	5	5.33	0.33

From ranking these projects in order of merit, we note the following important things:

1. The correct method of ranking the projects in order of merit is the present value approach.
2. The present value approach avoids the payback faults of (a) failing to consider cash flows after payback, and (b) failing to consider the time value of money.
3. If we have only $30 million available for funding capital investments, then we should fund project A ($13 million) and project C ($17 million) but not project B ($5 million). The situation of having a limited amount to fund the initial investment in capital projects is known as "capital rationing."

The Internal Rate of Return Method

The internal rate of return (IRR) method of evaluating capital investment projects is well and widely known. Therefore it must be mentioned here. However, having made the obligatory mention, let us ignore it. It has serious drawbacks, which demand a lot of attention and explanation – which are not necessary to explore, because we do not need the IRR. The PV method does everything that the IRR method does, and so we can do without the IRR, and lose nothing by ignoring it[6].

Chapter Summary

This chapter covered capital budgeting, which evaluates how to select which capital investment projects to fund, and which to reject, or defer. The topics covered are as follows:

1. The Payback Method.

---

[6] We also ignore the Modified Internal Rate of Return Method, (MIRR) which is closely related to the IRR Method.

2. The Present Value Method.
3. The Internal Rate of Return Method.
4. Capital Rationing

Practice Problems

1. Ajax Corporation is considering three capital investment projects, with the following cash flows in $ millions:

Year	Project A	Project B	Project C
0	-100	-120	-90
1 - 9	19		
1 - 12		25	
1- 15			13
Hurdle Rate	10%	14%	9%
Answer			
PV Inflows	109.42	141.51	104.79
Less Initial Investment	-100.00	-120.00	-90.00
Net PV	9.42	21.51	14.79
Rank	3	1	2

2. Same problem as #1 above, except that the cash inflows are now uneven, as shown below:

Year	Project A	Project B	Project C
0	-100	-120	-90
1 - 9	19	25	13
10 - 12	14	35	
10- 15			20
Hurdle Rate	10%	14%	9%
Answer			
PV Inflows*	122.84	145.58	115.84
Less Initial Investment	-100.00	-120.00	-90.00
Net PV	22.84	25.58	25.84
Rank	3	2	1

*The PV calculations require several steps due to the uneven cash inflows. For all 3 projects we first find the PV results for years 1-9. Then, for projects A and B we find the PV results for the 3 years 10-12, which gives us the PV as of the beginning of year 10[7]. The beginning of year 10 is equivalent to the end of year 9. So we regard our value at the end of year 9 as an FV, as of year 0. We use PV to convert this FV from year 9 to its PV in year 0. Finally, we add this PV to our PV for years 1-9, to get our total PV of cash inflows for all years. Here are the separate steps: check them out.

Year	Project A	Project B	Project C
0	-100	-120	-90
1 - 9	19	25	13
10 - 12	14	35	
10- 15			20
Hurdle Rate	10%	14%	9%
PV yrs1-9	109.42	123.66	77.94
PV yrs 10+	34.82	81.26	89.72
PV yr 0	13.42	21.92	37.90
PV inflows	122.84	145.58	115.84

---

[7] For project C it is the PV for the 6 years 10-15.

Chapter 6

Global Finance

The Internet is becoming the town square for the global village of tomorrow.

Bill Gates

This chapter describes the financial issues that confront companies who sell or operate facilities in other countries. These issues embrace culture, language, currency, and politics, as well as finance. Many large U.S. companies are multinational [8] , including Boeing, McDonalds, Caterpillar, Amazon, Microsoft, PepsiCo, and KFC, to name just a

---

[8] Multinational means having operations in more than one country.

few. By the same token, many companies based in other countries also operate in the USA, such as Bayer, Toyota, Shell Oil, BMW, Honda, Samsung, Nokia, and many more. All multinational companies face issues such as exchange rates.

Exchange Rates

Exchange rates are the terms on which one nation's currency can be exchanged for the currency of a different nation. For example, the U.S. dollar may be expressed in Canadian dollars, or Mexican pesos or Chinese yuan, or Japanese yen, or Indian rupee, or many other national currencies. The rates of exchange usually fluctuate, and can be checked at banks and online, at websites like the following:

1. http://www.oanda.com/
2. http://www.x-rates.com/
3. http://www.exchangerate.com/

Since rates of exchange fluctuate, there is also fluctuation in the amount of home currency that multinational companies receive when repatriating amounts earned in other countries.

For example, Toyota and BMW earn dollars by selling autos in the U.S. When they repatriate those dollars into Japanese and German currencies respectively, the fluctuating exchange rates between the $U.S. and the respective Japanese and German currencies determine how many yen and how many Euros they actually receive. If the yen is appreciating against the $U.S. then Toyota gains on the rate of exchange. However, if the euro is sinking versus the $U.S. then BMW loses on the rate of exchange. That is one reason that both BMW and Toyota manufacture motor vehicles in the USA for sale in the USA – in order to avoid the risks of foreign currency fluctuations.

Reducing Foreign Exchange Risk

We see that one way to avoid the risks of foreign currency fluctuations is to keep both cash inflows and cash outflows in the same currency. In that case, there is no need to convert from one currency to another.

Another way to reduce the risks of foreign currency fluctuations is to buy or sell forward exchange, as the case may be. For example, say an Iowa company agrees to sell wheat to a Russian company for Russian rubles two months from today. Not wanting to suffer the risks of the $U.S./ruble rate of exchange two months from today, the Iowa company can immediately convert its rubles due two months from today into $U.S. today.

In that way it avoids the risks of the $U.S./ruble rate of exchange two months from today. Instead, the risk is now transferred to the foreign exchange dealer who sold the forward exchange contract to the Iowa company. Of course, the foreign exchange dealer will aim to profit on the transaction. Therefore it will cost the Iowa company some money to transfer the currency risk to the foreign exchange dealer[9]. This cost will likely be reflected in the $U.S./ruble rate of exchange in the contract.

But each party to the contract still gains from the transaction. Without a gain, neither party would enter into the contract. The Iowa company has expertise in producing wheat, and is pleased to transfer the currency risk to the foreign exchange dealer, even though there is a cost for doing so. The foreign exchange dealer is pleased to accept the currency risk because the dealer is an expert in foreign exchange rates, and earns a fee for selling his skill and assuming the risk.

Purchasing Power Parity

---

[9] The transfer of foreign exchange risk is known as "hedging."

How does the foreign exchange dealer go about setting a foreign exchange rate in the forward exchange contract? Clearly no-one knows for sure what the future may hold. But there are ways to predict the future that are less than certain, but better than chance. One such approach is purchasing power parity.

The purchasing power parity theory[10] states that changes in exchange rates are related to changes in the price levels in the countries in question. The changes in the price levels are measured by comparing prices for a similar market basket of goods. The theory is based on the observation that countries with faster price increases than other countries will have lower exports and higher imports than other countries. Therefore the demand for the currency of countries with faster price increases than other countries will decline, and the demand for the currency of countries

---

[10] Specifically this is the relative rather than the absolute purchasing power parity theory.

with slower price increases than other countries will increase. In turn the currency of countries with faster price increases than other countries will depreciate, and the currency of countries with slower price increases than other countries will appreciate.

Of course, this theory is weakened by barriers to trade such as transportation costs, tariffs, customs duties, and other trade barriers. But despite this weakening, there is still considerable validity to the theory. Also, governments may intervene in the foreign exchange markets. Such intervention can have appreciable impact, but also it is difficult to move large markets. So even despite government intervention, the purchasing power parity theory still remains substantially valid.

Inflation Expectations

Changes in the purchasing power of money are known as inflation (or deflation, as the case may be). Earlier we established that inflation was a component of interest rates. In specific terms, we noted that all interest rates contained allowances for:

1. Delaying consumption;
2. Inflation;
3. Risk.

The allowance for delaying consumption is more or less constant regardless of the prospects of inflation and the risk expectations involved. Therefore differences in interest rates relate mostly to differences in expected inflation and in expected risks for the period in question. In general, long-term interest rates are higher than short-term interest rates. The reason is that the long-term is regarded as more risky than the short-term, and expected inflation may differ with respect to the long-term and the short-term.

If we can find two different interest rates of similar risk, then the difference between them is probably due to the difference in expected inflation.

For example, if the annual interest rate on one-year U.S. treasuries is 1.5% and the annual interest rate on ten-year U.S. treasuries is 3.5% we know that the annual difference of 2% cannot be due to delaying consumption or risk because both securities are risk-free.

Therefore this 2% difference is due to the higher expected annual rate of inflation over the 10-year period than the 1-year period. So we have the market consensus on expected inflation over the next 10 years. Of course, this is just an expectation, and it may turn out to be wrong, because no-one knows the future. But it is still a useful forecast, and it is the best available forecast because it is the consensus forecast of the entire market.

The main point that we have learned is that rates of foreign exchange are largely influenced by relative inflation in the respective countries. The expected rates of inflation can be forecasted by the careful use of interest rates. Therefore future expected rates of foreign exchange can also be forecasted. Note that these forecasts are less than certain, because the future cannot be known. But although less than certain, these future expected rates of foreign exchange are much better than nothing. Of course, future expected rates of foreign exchange are by no means the only risks of global finance.

Cultural Risk

Multinational companies operate in countries with differing cultures. These various cultural factors can affect company operations in numerous ways. There are many languages, customs, totems and taboos to be aware of. For instance, the Chevy Nova was not a big success in Hispanic countries, because in Spanish "no va" means "won't go." In some countries, bribes are routinely expected gratuities in order to get many things done, but are prohibited by the U.S. Foreign Corrupt Practices Act of 1978.

There are endless examples of such culture traps for the unwary. It therefore is vital for all multinational companies to carefully train employees in the cultures of host countries so that employees can conduct business in an accepted manner and not create resentment or riots in areas to which they are not native.

Political Risk

In addition to foreign exchange and cultural risks, multinational companies also must contend with political risk. Political risk stems from government interventions such as asset freezes, blocked repatriation of funds, the expropriation (confiscation) of company assets, (with or without compensation), regulations requiring local content or employment of local workers, or a host of other impositions by the host governments.

Having summarized the foreign exchange risks, cultural risks, and political risks of

Finance Made Easy (2nd Edition)
global business, how are these risks dealt with in global finance?

Compensating for All Global Risks

In an earlier chapter we described computing the required rate of return as practiced in a domestic setting. Now we extend the required rate of return to a global basis. The process for computing the domestic required rate of return is:

WACC
Add adjustment for projects with no cash inflows.
Add allowance for risk of project type
Hurdle rate for project

When a foreign project is concerned, this process is longer, as follows:

WACC
Add adjustment for projects with no cash inflows.
Add allowance for risk of project type
Add allowance for foreign exchange risk
Add allowance for cultural risks
Add allowance for political risks
Hurdle rate for project

Finance Made Easy (2nd Edition)

<u>Chapter Summary</u>

This chapter included the following topics:

1. Rates of Foreign Exchange.
2. Reducing Exchange Rate Risk.
3. Purchasing Power Parity.
4. Forecasting Expected Inflation.
5. Compensating for the Risks of:
     a. Culture.
     b. Politics
6. Compensating for All Global Risks.

<u>Practice Problems</u>

1. Citrix Corporation is a U.S. company that owns an effective new patented process for making orange juice. Citrix has entered into a joint venture with Naranja, a Brazilian company to build a processing plant in Brazil to use oranges grown by Naranja in order to produce orange juice. Under the joint venture agreement, Naranja will supply the oranges without

charge while Citrix will pay the entire cost of building the processing plant. The product will be sold in the U.S. and Brazil. Profits before income tax will be shared equally by Citrix and Naranja. Citrix has a WACC of 9%. Citrix capital investment projects with no cash inflows are funded by 10% of its capital structure, and include both pollution reduction and safety equipment.

Information on Brazil and its economy can be found online at:
1. http://www.heritage.org/index/Country/Brazil
2. https://www.cia.gov/library/publications/the-world-factbook/geos/br.html
3. http://www.dismal.com/dismal/country_pages.asp?geo=IBRA

Assignment: estimate the hurdle rate for this capital investment project. Answer: allowance should be made for the following factors listed below.

Amounts for each factor are estimated as Best Case and Worst Case, due to the inherent uncertainty involved:

Factor	Calculations	Best Case	Worst Case
WACC	Given	9.0%	9.0%
Adjustment for projects with no cash inflows.	9% x 100/90	1.0%	1.0%
Allowance for risk of project type	Existing item new market	2.0%	4.0%
Allowance for foreign exchange risk	Using oanda.com website	1.0%	3.0%
Allowance for cultural risks	Using CIA World Factbook	1.0%	3.0%
Allowance for political risks	Using Heritage Fdn Index of Economic Freedom	1.0%	3.0%
Hurdle rate for project		15.0%	23.0%

2. Annual profits for the above joint venture are estimated to be 12 million BRL (Brazilian real) per year for 10 years. The initial cost of the plant is estimated to be 18 million BRL. Brazilian corporate tax is 30%, and U.S. corporate tax is 35% on all corporate income repatriated to the U.S. Citrix expects to repatriate all its income. U.S. tax allows a tax credit for all foreign tax paid. What is the net present value to Citrix of this project? Answer: the annual cash inflows are as follows:

Annual	BRL (million)
Pretax Profit	12.00
Citrix 50%	6.00
Brazil Tax	1.80
Citrix Profit After Tax	4.20
U.S. Tax	0.00
Citrix Cash Inflow	4.20

Exchange Rate 1.6 BRL Per $U.S.	BRL million	$U.S. million
Citrix Annual Cash Inflow	4.20	6.72
Initial Investment	18.0	28.8

Variable	Best Case	Worst Case
RATE	15%	23%
NPER	10	10
PMT $ million	6.72	6.72
PV Inflows $ million	33.73	25.53
Initial Investment $ million	28.80	28.80
Net Present Value $ million	4.93	-3.27

Our results are mixed. The good news is that the Best Case net present value is positive. The bad news is that the Worst Case net present value is negative. Citrix has received a warning signal, and it would be dangerous to ignore this red flag and to approve the capital investment project.

Finance Made Easy (2nd Edition)
Author Background

LES LIVINGSTONE earned MBA and Ph.D. degrees at
Stanford University and is a CPA (licensed in NY and TX).
Since 1991 he has directed his own consulting firm which
specializes in Damage Estimation for large-scale Commercial
Litigation and in Business Valuation. He has served as a
Consulting or Testifying Expert in many cases, including
Breach of Contract, Patent Infringement, Fraudulent
Conveyance, Antitrust, Dealer Termination, Franchise
Disputes, and Securities Fraud. He has testified in Federal and
State courts in Arizona, California, Florida, Georgia, Illinois,
Massachusetts, New York, Rhode Island, and Texas, and he
has also testified before Federal government agencies
including the FTC, FERC, as well as the Public Utilities
Commission of Texas.

Experience in accounting, finance and business includes:

- Babson College: Professor of Accounting and Chairman,
  Division of Accounting & Law.

- The MAC Group (now Cap Gemini/Ernst & Young
  Consulting), an international management consulting firm
  specializing in design and implementation of business
  strategy for major corporations: Principal.

- Coopers & Lybrand (now PricewaterhouseCoopers),

Finance Made Easy (2nd Edition)

Partner.

*   Georgia Institute of Technology: Fuller E. Callaway Professor of Accounting.

*   Ohio State University: Arthur Young Distinguished Professor of Accounting.

Publications: Author or coauthor of:

*   About 50 articles in leading professional journals.

*   Numerous chapters in authoritative handbooks.

*   19 books.

*   Recent books include: Economics Made Easy (2nd edition, 2011), Common Sense (2011), Public Choice (2010), Ethical Decision Making (2nd edition 2010), Guide to Business Valuation (2007) and "The Portable MBA in Finance and Accounting" (4th edition, 2009), a selection of the Book of the Month Club, the Fortune Book Club and the Money Book Club. Later, the paperback edition was a selection of the Quality Paperback Book Club. Translated into Chinese, French, Indonesian, Japanese, Portuguese, Russian and Spanish.